FRIENDSHIP

Ralph Waldo Emerson

Illustrated by
Richard Allen

SOUVENIR PRESS

I awoke this morning with devout thanksgiving for my friends, the old and the new.

I do not wish to treat friendships daintily, but with roughest courage. When they are real, they are not glass threads or frostwork, but the solidest thing we know. The sweet sincerity of joy and peace, which I draw from this alliance with my brother's soul, is the nut itself, whereof all nature and all thought is but the husk and shell.

HAPPY is the house that shelters a friend! It might well be built, like a festal bower or arch, to entertain him a single day. Happier, if he know the solemnity of that relation, and honour its law! He who offers himself a candidate for that covenant comes up, like an Olympian to the great games, where the first-born of the world are the competitors.

A friend is a person with whom I may be sincere. Before him I may think aloud. I am arrived at last in the presence of a man so real and equal, that I may drop even those undermost garments of dissimulation, courtesy, and second thought, which men never put off, and may deal with him with the simplicity and wholeness with which one chemical atom meets another.

ALMOST every man we meet requires some civility—requires to be humoured. But a friend is a sane man who exercises not my ingenuity, but me. My friend gives me entertainment without requiring any stipulation on my part. A friend, therefore, is a sort of paradox in nature.

I who alone *am*, I who see nothing in nature whose existence I can affirm with equal evidence to my own, behold now the semblance of my being, in all its height, variety, and curiosity, reiterated in a foreign form; so that a friend may well be reckoned the masterpiece of nature.

THE other element of friendship is tenderness. We are holden to men by every sort of tie, but we can scarce believe that so much character can subsist in another as to draw us by love. When a man becomes dear to me, I have touched the goal of fortune.

THE end of friendship is a commerce the most strict and homely that can be joined; more strict than any of which we have experience. It is for aid and comfort through all the relations and passages of life and death. It is fit for serene days, and graceful gifts, and country rambles, but also for rough roads and hard fare, shipwreck, poverty, and persecution. It keeps company with the sallies of the wit and the trances of religion.

It should never fall into something usual and settled, but should be alert and inventive, and add rhyme and reason to what was drudgery.

FRIENDSHIP requires that rare mean betwixt likeness and unlikeness, that piques each with the presence of power and of consent in the other party. Let me be alone to the end of the world, rather than that my friend should overstep, by a word or a look, his real sympathy. Let him not cease an instant to be himself. Better be a nettle in the side of your friend than his echo.

FRIENDSHIP demands a religious treatment. We talk of choosing our friends, but friends are self-elected. Reverence is a great part of it. Treat your friend as a spectacle.

OF course he has merits that are not yours, and that you cannot honour, if you must needs hold him close to your person. Stand aside; give those merits room; let them mount and expand. Are you the friend of your friend's buttons, or his thought? To a great heart he will still be a stranger in a thousand particulars, that he may come near in the holiest ground.

WHAT is so great as friendship, let us carry with what grandeur of spirit we can. Let us be silent—so we may hear the whisper of the gods. Let us not interfere. Wait, and thy heart shall speak. Wait until the necessary and everlasting overpowers you, until day and night avail themselves of your lips. The only reward of virtue is virtue; the only way to have a friend is to be one.

It is foolish to be afraid of making our ties too spiritual, as if so we could lose any genuine love. Let us even bid our dearest friends farewell, and defy them, saying, 'I will be dependent no more.' Thus we part only to meet again on a higher platform, and only be more each other's, because we are more our own. A friend is Janus-faced: he looks to the past and the future. He is the child of all my foregoing hours, the prophet of those to come, and the harbinger of a greater friend.

THE essence of friendship is entireness, a total magnanimity and trust. It must not surmise or provide for infirmity. It treats its object as a god, that it may deify both.

Dedicated to the Memory of
ALEC HARRISON

ISBN 0 285 62843 7

Photoset, printed and bound in Great Britain by
Redwood Burn Limited,
Trowbridge, Wiltshire